Black Women in WWII: Greatness Under Fire

By Dante R. Brizill

Publisher: KDP

Cover and design: Robert Gussio

Editor: Nancy Samuels

Ordering information: This book may be published in large quantities for educational use. For additional copies or information, email at dbrizill@icloud.com.

Request Dante

To request Dante R. Brizill for a keynote address, speaking engagement, workshop, or seminar, contact Ray Feldmann at Ray@fcstrategies.com.

Like the Facebook page Black Women in WWII: Greatness Under Fire

"A woman is free if she lives by her own standards and creates her own destiny, if she prizes her individuality and puts no boundaries on her hopes for tomorrow."

– ***Mary McLeod Bethune***

Table of Contents

Author's Note

Researching and writing the *"Greatness Under Fire"* series, has allowed me to uncover so many hidden gems of African American men and women who contributed to our victory in World War II. It has been a rewarding experience. I started with the son of Texas sharecroppers in the person of Doris "Dorie" Miller, who was one of our first heroes in World War II. *Dorie Miller: Greatness Under Fire* details his heroic actions at Pearl Harbor. I followed up with *Red Ball Express: Greatness Under Fire* about a largely African American group of truck drivers that delivered essential supplies to the American armies during a key time period in the war. Both of these stories are not widely taught or well-known apart from the World War II buff. It is time for our young people to be introduced to these heroes and see themselves when World War II is taught in their United States history classes. As I conclude this series, it is fitting to end with the role that black women played in the struggle. African American women fought courageously for the right to participate in helping to win the war. Mostly confined to domestic work and agricultural jobs prior to the war, World War II gave them an opportunity to rise above the limits a segregated society placed on them. One of the reasons that the United States contributed mightily to the Allied victory in World War II was its ability to out produce the opposition and replace losses quickly. This would not have been possible without the enormous role that women played on the homefront. The "Black Rosies" are a part of that story.

In many ways when doing the research for this book, I was reminded of the women in the movie *Hidden Figures* who helped make our space program a success in the early 1960's. One of the highlights of my teaching career was the opportunity to take two busloads of students to see this movie with several of my colleagues, and afterwards having a female student remark that she would try harder in her math class and not be so quick to give up. The women mentioned in this book no doubt paved the way for these women in *Hidden Figures*.

In WWII, African-Americans had to fight two wars: Nazi Germany and Imperial Japan overseas and racism at home. In response to a letter from a 26-year old African-American cafeteria worker in Kansas, the legendary black newspaper, the *Pittsburgh Courier*, initiated the "Double V" campaign: victory over fascism overseas and racism at home. Segregation at home would face new challenges to stay afloat; this extended to the rigidly segregated military and defense industry. Membership in civil rights organizations multiplied during the war. The battle scars to make WWII an equal fight for all Americans laid the groundwork for the Civil Rights Movement of the 1950's and 60's.

What fire did African American women face in WWII as the title of this book suggests? The fire they faced was resistance to their even being allowed to participate. As this book will show, black women had to fight to work in the factories that produced the war materials needed for victory. Black women were usually hired as a last resort when white female and black male labor was maximized. They had to fight to be admitted into the WAC's, even a segregated one, and to serve as nurses for our wounded. It is important for the reader to understand that in 1940's America, no federal law compelled employers to hire regardless of a person's race. Federal agencies had little authority outside of persuasion to compel employers to have fair employment practices. The country was still over two decades away from banning employment discrimination based on race and gender when the United States entered World War II. This makes the story of these women and the barriers they had to break down even more extraordinary. They overcame these challenges and served with distinction. They were trailblazers for their daughters and granddaughters that followed. When doors were closed to them, they persisted. This book details several powerful stories that demonstrate their courage and greatness under fire.

The mainstream media at the time pretty much ignored the role and participation of black women at home and overseas and almost exclusively focused on white women as evidenced by the iconic "Rosie the Riveter" poster. A careful examination of World War II home-front propaganda makes the black woman almost invisible. But, in reality, nothing could be further from the truth. Black newspapers, periodicals, memoirs, letters, diaries, and photographers left us with a wealth of knowledge about their role. The fact of the matter is America needed the full participation of every group of Americans to win the war. The government and the war industry slowly came to the conclusion that racial segregation could be counterproductive to the war industry and the moral authority of a country fighting fascism and Nazism. This did lead to some doors being open to black women, but full racial equality was still a generation away. The price they paid for the door being cracked slightly was lower pay, often menial work, the night shift and the least desirable jobs that often was well below their qualifications and training. Still they persisted. They left a template for their daughters to perfect and follow in the years ahead.

This book in no way chronicles every single contribution black women made in WWII, but I chose to focus on several powerful stories in a concise way to inspire and encourage the reader to pursue greatness. You will learn about women who are not household names or adorn the pages of your high school history textbook. This book should serve as a starting point and an introduction to find out more about the role and achievements of African-American women in WWII.

Dedication

To the African American women who served our country in World War II at home and abroad. You are not forgotten. You helped win a war. May history give you the due that you have earned. May you be included in the narrative and no longer subject to the margins of history or ignored in any public school curriculum. May your descendants continue to tell your stories to their children and grandchildren. They must no longer be hidden.

How to Use this Book

This book can be used in conjunction with an American history unit on World War II. It can serve as an enrichment piece to the established curriculum. Prior background knowledge of the contributions of American civilians on the home front along with knowledge of American involvement and entry into World War II would be helpful and would provide much needed context for students. In addition to that, it is also helpful to understand the impact of Jim Crow laws in early to mid-20th century America and the barriers this presented to equality. In addition to that, this book could serve as a useful resource in gender studies and the impact that World War II had on the changing role of women.

Introduction

The year is 1941. Mary is an African American woman working as a domestic. She is paid $7.00 a week. Her duties include cooking, laundry and housekeeping. Shc has friends who make a lot less, but she knows her salary isn't great either. Her mother and grandmother did this kind of work too; however, Mary did not want this to be her future. If it wasn't for her husband's salary as a janitor, she believes they and their two children would be out on the streets.

One day as she was working in her host family's kitchen preparing breakfast, she happened upon an advertisement in the local paper. It had been left on the kitchen table by the man of the house. The advertisement mentioned that workers were needed at the local defense plant. Women were wanted too. From neighbors and church gossip, Mary knew what the going rate for defense work was. She knew that she could more than double her pay walking out of that kitchen onto a factory floor. Therefore, she decided that before her shift started the next day, she would show up and express interest in person. She knew exactly where the plant was located because she had to pass it on her way to the bus stop to get to her domestic job. Mary was excited! Tomorrow she would wear her new shoes, that took her a whole month to save up for, and her Sunday dress.

The next day she knocked on the door of the plant and was coldly greeted by the receptionist. *"May I help you?'* the receptionist said to her rudely.

"Oh yes. I am interested in working here. I saw an ad in the paper that you were hiring," Mary responded.

"We already have a cleaning lady that comes here several times a week. And our cafeteria isn't hiring at this time. Have a good day now!"

"But I'm not interested in being your cleaning lady or cook ma'am," Mary responded impatiently. "This is a defense plant, and that's the kind of work I'm asking about."

The receptionist eyed Mary up and down for a good 30 seconds before responding.

"Sit down, gal, for a minute and let me talk to Sam," the receptionist instructed her.

Mary noticed that the receptionist went into another office behind hers and shut the door. She could make out part of what was being said.

"This colored gal is out here inquiring about working here. I told her we don't need no cooks or cleaning ladies!"

Mary heard the man chuckle before responding to the receptionist, *"She saw that ad we've been running in the paper. Tell her the position has been filled."*

Then Mary heard them both laugh. The receptionist continued, *"Who do they think they are anyway? Thinking they can come up here and do white people's work?*

The receptionist came back out into the seating area and said, *"My boss just informed me that the position has been filled. Sorry, gal. Have a good day now.*"

This story is based on actual events. Mary represents the dilemma that African American women found themselves in as the United States entered World War II. This book will explore how these women conquered these barriers and how they contributed to our victory in the war. It is my hope that as you read this book, you will be inspired to master every stumbling block thrown in your path that would block your success.

Black Rosie's are Ready for Duty

When the United States entered World War II on December 8th, 1941, following the Japanese attack the day before, the country had to abruptly revert to a war footing that would require millions of soldiers to serve and millions more at home to work in the war industries. After experiencing the Great Depression in the 1930's in which millions of Americans faced lack, poverty, and hunger on a massive scale, the war provided a role for everyone. Despite segregation and discrimination based on race, African Americans were determined that during this conflict they would demand their fair share and would be treated equally before the law. Many of these goals were not met during the war years, but progress did come in small steps; the seeds were planted for the progress yet to come.

The term "Rosie" refers to the 20 million women who went to work in defense industries and factories to complete jobs that were done by men. As men were drafted and enlisted in the war, women filled these important jobs. African-American women wanted a share of these jobs.

As we saw in the opening story of Mary trying to find a job, African American women did not passively accept slammed doors in their faces. Even when they had completed the same training as their white counterparts, companies often refused to hire them. Some would only agree to hire them as cleaning ladies (which we saw that Mary refused to take) or limited them exclusively to the night shift. Two real-life women decided to challenge this assumption that insulted their abilities: Effie Mae Turner and Claretta Johnson.

Turner and Johnson were highly skilled and qualified women who completed a vigorous amount of preparation for war jobs. Turner even completed 240 hours of training. Johnson sued a major aircraft manufacturing company over job discrimination. Both women believed that their race hindered them from being hired. Their cases eventually went all the way to the Ohio Supreme Court which ruled against them. But in the decades to come, the courts would be an essential battleground in the fight for racial equality.

Often times once the factory doors were open, African American women faced resistance from colleagues who thought it was insulting to work with them. Sometimes white workers walked off the job to protest the hiring of black women. One such incident in Maryland caused President Roosevelt to intervene.

At the Western Electric Company in Baltimore, Maryland, over 1,000 union employees voted to strike when the company refused to provide separate toilet facilities for black and white women. This company was under contract to provide the government with war supplies. This disruption caused the president to send in the US Army to seize control of the plant to keep the production going.

Work stoppages were not something that could be tolerated during war, as the government assumed emergency powers. As blacks became a bigger part of the workforce during the war, and as millions moved north to find jobs in the defense industries, racial tensions increased. In Philadelphia in 1944 when eight black transportation workers were promoted to positions of trolley driver, hundreds of Philadelphia Transit Employees went on strike to protest. People who relied on public transportation could not get to work. This was a serious threat to the war effort. It was so much of a problem, that President Roosevelt had to send in federal troops to the city in order to end it.

Below is my article on the contribution of "Black Rosies" in World War II that ran on Memorial Day 2021 in the *Philadelphia Inquirer.* Reprinted with permission from the *Philadelphia Inquirer*:

Memorial Day gives us an opportunity to pay our respects and honor the men and women who made the ultimate sacrifice for the freedoms that we enjoy today. World War II was our largest and costliest wars. It was during this war that African Americans demanded full participation on a scale that had not been seen before.

As America went to war to fight Imperial Japan and Nazi Germany, African Americans answered the call on factory floors, in shipyards, and at recruiting offices across America-a country that treated them as second classed citizens and little more than manual labor robots. But as a price for their service, they demanded equal justice under the law as well as the opportunity to be treated fairly. Serving as defense workers, nurses, and WACs (Women's Army Corps), the story of African American women deserves our heartfelt appreciation every Memorial Day.

Being Black and a woman in the 1940s was a double whammy that presented its own unique obstacles and dangers to navigate. Black women found few opportunities beyond domestic work or toiling in cotton fields under the rigid system of sharecropping in the early decades of the 20th century. World War II accelerated the migration of African Americans out of the agrarian South to the industrial North. The war opened doors for them that in many cases they had to pry open and put down door stoppers to keep open.

By 1941, the American war industry was kicking into high gear as the United States supplied Britain and the Soviet Union critical war supplies under the Lend-Lease Act. Sensing the importance of keeping these two nations in the war against Germany, Roosevelt persuaded Congress to provide this critical aid. After over a decade of economic depression, WWII arguably was the best jobs program in American history, bringing the unemployment rate down to almost zero by 1944. The problem for many African Americans was that the defense industries openly discriminated against them.

Civil rights activists such as Mary McLeod Bethune and A. Phillip Randolph brought to President Franklin Roosevelt's attention these unfair practices. Randolph even threatened a march on Washington. Knowing the huge public relations disaster this could bring on the United States, Randolph's threat compelled Roosevelt to sign Executive Order 8802 which banned racial discrimination in the defense industry. Even though the order had very little enforcement power, it did open the door to one million African American workers — 600,000 of them women.

Mary McLeod Bethune and First Lady Eleanor Roosevelt both pictured in the center celebrate the opening of a residence hall for "Negro government girls" in 1943. (*National Archives*)

Known as "Black Rosies" and often assigned the dirtiest jobs, Black women worked in factories doing sheet metal work, as assemblers of munitions and explosives, as well as in shipyards, railroads, and administrative offices. Despite these advances, women workers in general were paid less than men, with Black women being the lowest compensated. Some factories still stubbornly refused to hire African Americans and, in some cases, white workers walked off the job to protest their presence.

Working in the war industries paid well. A typical domestic worker made roughly $7 per week. In southern states it was as low as $3 to $4 a week. War jobs paid as much as $35 a week. African American women jumped at this chance. Many spoke fondly of their service on the home-front and their contribution to American victory in World War II. As Ruth Wilson, one of the "Black Rosies" from Philadelphia, exclaimed, "It made me feel good because my husband was over there in Europe fighting, and here I was doing my part."

21-year old Bertha Stallworth inspects ammunition cartridges. (*National Archives)*

African American women also were admitted into the Women's Army Corps after the insistence of First Lady Eleanor Roosevelt and Mary McLeod Bethune. Segregation would still be the prevailing policy, but out of this policy came the storied 6888th Central Postal Directory Battalion.

In February 1945, the first part of this battalion sailed for England. They faced an important mission. There was a backlog of undelivered mail of more than 17 million letters and packages to be sorted through and delivered to the appropriate serviceman. The women understood how important receiving letters was to the morale of the troops, with their motto being "No mail, low morale."

As we recognize and memorialize the sacrifices that our men and women in uniform made, let us never forget the important contributions of the "Black Rosies."

Welders on the *SS George Washington Carver* in 1943.

(*National Archives*)

Major Charity Adams inspects her unit somewhere in England. (*National Archives)*

The 6888th Central Postal Directory Battalion

Receiving a letter from home from a loved one was a big deal to our troops serving in World War II as in all of our armed conflicts. A letter from home could lift the spirits of a war weary soldier. When there was a backlog of millions of pieces of mail along with undelivered Christmas packages, the skilled and talented women of the 6888th Central Postal Directory Battalion came to the rescue.

As part of the **WAC** (Women's Auxillary Corp), the 6888th Central Postal Directory Battalion was an all African American female unit created in 1944. **Major Charity Adams** was selected to command the unit. The daughter of a minister and a school teacher, Adams certainly was a history making person in a couple of ways. She was the first Black woman to be commissioned as an officer and the highest ranking one in the war. Prior to her service in WWII, Charity Adams was the valedictorian of her high school graduating class at Booker T. Washington High in Columbia, South Carolina. She was two years younger than her classmates after having started school in the second grade. This achievement allowed her to gain a scholarship to Wilburforce University a Historically Black College in Ohio where she majored in math, Latin, and physics while minoring in history. After graduating with a Bachelor of Arts in 1938, she taught math and science in Columbia, South Carolina. In 1942 the Women's Army Corps was created. First lady **Eleanor Roosevelt** along with educator and civil rights leader **Mary McLeod Bethune** were successful in pushing for African American women to be accepted into the program. As early as 1942, Bethune made speeches encouraging Black women to join the Women's Army Auxiliary Corps, explaining that this experience would open doors for them in career fields such as nursing and teaching. Bethune and Colonel Oveta Culp Hobby targeted colleges as well in search of names. Adams decided to apply to the program and was accepted. She trained at the officer training school at Fort Des Moines in Iowa; she was commissioned on August 29, 1942.

Charity Adams was familiar with segregation in her native South Carolina, but was shocked to see that this was how the military operated too. After her first meal in the military, a young white officer ordered all of the African American women to "move over on this side". He then began to tell the shocked women that separate housing had been provided to black and white recruits. After graduating from basic training on August 30th, 1942, she made history by becoming the first black woman to be commissioned into the WAAC, when she was made company commander of the female Basic Training Company. Her job was to transform the civilian women into military life and culture; she excelled.

By the end of 1944, she was chosen to command the 6888th Central Postal Directory Battalion. As previously documented, Major Adams was a trailblazer, but this did not exempt her from being reminded of her gender and color and the subservient role in which she was expected to operate. In January of 1944, she was invited to an officer's club in Iowa for a drink by another white officer. Her superior officer got wind of this and chewed her out in a lengthy tirade. He angrily reminded her that she needed to stay "in her place."

Major Adams Earley arrived in London in January of 1945, with sealed orders where she learned that she would command the 688th Central Postal Battalion.

By February of 1945, the first group from the battalion arrived in England. After surviving Nazi U-boats and an explosion from a German V-1 rocket, the women traveled by train to Birmingham, England. Known as the "Six Triple Eight," these women had a monumental task ahead of them.

Once the women arrived in Birmingham, England they had some problems to solve. When Major Adams addressed the women after their 11-day journey across the Atlantic dodging German U-boats, she made it clear to them that she would put them to work immediately. First and foremost was how to get the 17 million packages and letters that were stacked up to the ceiling in these warehouses out to our men in uniform in a timely and orderly fashion. How would they perform such a task in poorly lit and unheated buildings with rats seeking out spoiled food in the packages? What the women did not know was that the whole concept of their unit was an experiment, to see if black women were up to the task at hand. Major Adams knew this, and with the organization and skill of the school teacher she once was, she brilliantly set up her unit to be successful; they responded with a job well done.

The women wore extra layers of clothing under their coats to stay warm as they worked in the warehouses. In order to speed up the process, the women were organized in three separate eight-hour shifts around the clock for seven days a week. They came up with a tracking system of around seven million information cards with serial numbers to distinguish service members with the same name. They had to deal with returning mail to families of soldiers that had died as well as with anything that was sent to the wrong address. While processing this mail, they had to figure out the handwriting which could be difficult to understand as well as repackage packages that were falling apart. Amazingly with the tracking system they developed, the women processed an average of 65,000 pieces of mail per shift and cleared a six-month backlog in three months!

As hard as she worked her unit, she also protected them. Once when an army general inspected her unit, some of the women were working and sleeping at the time. The general threatened to remove Major Adams and replace her with a white officer. She refused to back down and made it known that she would be replaced "over my dead body." She remained the commander of her unit.

Major Adams drills her unit at Fort Des Moines in Iowa. (Source: *National Archives*)

Unfortunately, the racism and sexism that the women experienced at home in the United States were imported to England. African American WACs were not allowed entry into the recreational facilities set up by the American Red Cross nor the WAC hotels in London administered by them. Their leader, Major Charity Adams, refused to allow her unit to participate at any alternative sites nor in segregated units; therefore, in response, the women set up their own facilities to provide food, refreshments, and recreation. Many were even invited into English homes for tea. African American men and women noticed that white English civilians treated them more or less as equals compared to the treatment they received at home.

After performing such a great job in England, the women of the 6888th Central Postal Directory Battalion were shipped off to France in June of 1945. Upon their arrival in Le Havre, they were shocked at the devastation they saw that was left by the Nazis. From there the women took a train to Rouen and were housed in old French barracks. Upon their arrival, they learned that the building had been used by Nazi's during their occupation of France. Surrounded by high walls, the women attracted a lot of attention from the local population, as well as from the black and white soldiers. Apparently seeing a black woman in uniform could create a spectacle in 1945.

On a sad note, while in Rouen, the unit lost several of their members in a jeep accident. Their names were PFC Mary J. Barlow, PFC Mary H. Bankston, and Sergeant Delores M. Browne. Since the war department did not cover funeral expenses, the women of the unit pooled their resources to ensure that their fellow sisters would receive proper funerals and burials. They are buried in the American cemetery at Colleville-sur-Mer in Normandy.

After doing such an exemplary job with clearing the mail in Rouen, the women were sent to Paris where they were quartered in nice hotels and enjoyed quality food. By February of 1946, the entire unit was returned to the United States and disbanded at Fort Dix, New Jersey.

Members of the 6888th Central Postal Directory Battalion take part in a parade in France. African American women in Europe during WWII certainly could draw a crowd (Source: *National Archives*)

The 6888th Central Postal Directory Battalion did not receive a rousing welcome home ceremony, but they proved, according to a study done about the WACs in December of 1945, that the "*national security program is the joint responsibility of all Americans irrespective of color and sex.*" This outstanding unit opened doors for African American women in the military. The legacy of their service still resonates to this day.

After the war Adams left the service after being promoted to Lt. Colonel. The National Council of Negro Women named her Woman of the Year in 1946.

The heroic women of the famed "Six Triple Eight" continue to make news to this day. On February 11,2021 Congresswoman Gwen L. Moore (D-WI) introduced the "Six Triple Eight" Congressional Gold Medal Act of 2021. The goal was for the House of Representatives to have it passed by Veterans Day. On February 12,2021, US Senator Jerry Moran (R-KS) introduced similar legislation in the Senate. In April of 2021, the Senate passed the bill unanimously.

Arlington National Cemetery is where the heroes of our wars are buried. Row after row of white marble headstones mark the final resting place of these warriors. This sacred ground includes 14 of the over 800 women that served in the 6888th Central Postal Directory Battalion. What a fitting tribute to these women to lie in eternal rest with heroes!

Members of the 6888th enjoying a meal in England. (Source National Archives)

Black Nurses in WWII

Black women served as nurses as far back as the Civil War in convalescent homes and in U.S. government run hospitals. One of the most well-known was Harriet Tubman. Among the many endeavors that Harriet Tubman was involved in, she also served in numerous hospitals and applied remedies she remembered from childhood. Sojourner Truth worked in Union hospitals during the Civil War as well. African American nurses served in the Spanish-American war and helped to deal with the yellow fever and typhoid epidemics in the military. When America entered World War I in 1917, their service was not accepted by the military until some were sent to a few military camps in the U.S. to assist with the influenza pandemic. With American involvement in World War II beginning in 1941, African American nurses had to fight and push to be given a chance to help their nation attend to our wounded and sick servicemen.

Segregation, which was the prevailing policy of the military and much of America in 1941, unfortunately extended into the Army Nurse Corps. Thousands of black women filled out applications to serve, only to receive this demeaning response:

> Your application to the Army Nurse Corps cannot be given favorable consideration as there are no provisions in Army regulations for the appointment of colored nurses in the corps.

Mabel K. Staupers, who was the executive secretary of the National Association of Colored Graduate Nurses lobbied for a change in the policy. First Lady Eleanor Roosevelt also lobbied the army surgeon general to admit black nurses to the Army Nurse Corps. After this pressure was applied, the army finally allowed a limited number (56) to join using a strict quota system.

Black nurses arrive in Scotland in 1944. *(National Archives)*

As the war continued, the number of black nurses *did* increase, tripling by May of 1943. Restricted to segregated hospitals and aid stations, black nurses served in Africa, Burma, Australia, and England. One of the units that deployed to Africa was the 25th Station Hospital Unit. This unit contained thirty nurses. They were sent to Liberia to care for U.S. troops who were protecting airfields and the large rubber plantations owned by an American company. This company supplied America and its allies the rubber needed in the war. The most serious problem the nurses encountered was malaria.

One of the most humiliating tasks that African American nurses were assigned to do was to care for German POWs (prisoners of war). Thousands of them were sent to the United States during the war. In fact, over 300,000 were scattered across the United States in over 600 camps. Many African American nurses saw this task as a slap in the face. As noted earlier, it was very difficult for African American nurses to even be allowed to serve, so to be told that they would be caring for enemy soldiers who fought under the racist Nazi flag added insult to injury. Many of the German POWs did not need much medical care, so the skills of black nurses were underutilized. They cared for these prisoners in England and in the United

States. Many of these camps were located in the south and in the southwest part of the country which subjected black nurses to segregation and denial of service in local restaurants and businesses, services that were not denied to enemy POW's which was even documented in letters written by black soldiers stationed in the United States. Indeed, many German POW's were shocked to see how blacks were treated in the United States, as they had to make long journeys on the train to their assigned camps. This afforded them a front row seat to the daily humiliation that African-Americans passengers and workers had to endure in 1940's America. The black nurses that did not service POW's were sent to segregated military bases to aid black soldiers.

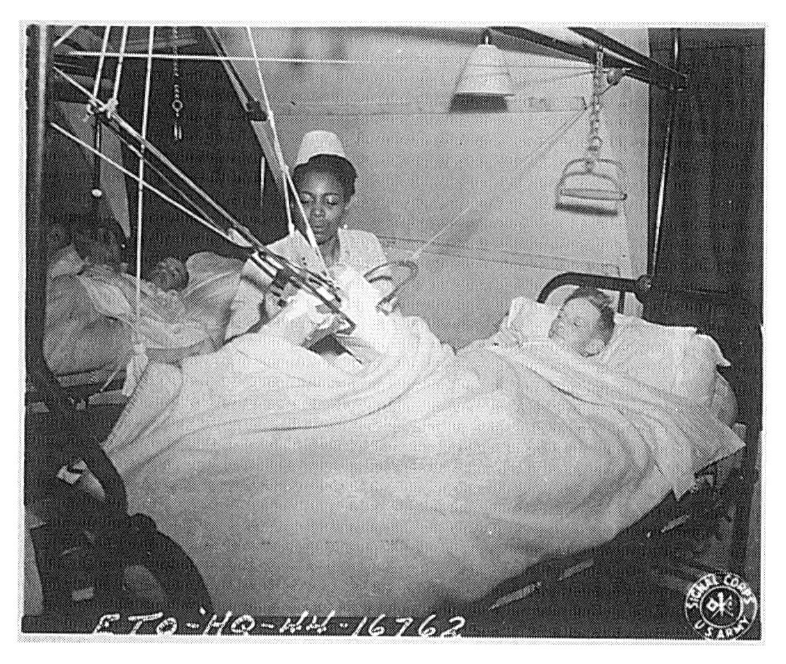

Nurse caring for a POW somewhere in England. (Source: *National Archives.)*

The last year of World War II saw the rise of casualties among American servicemen. Germany and Japan were close to defeat, even though they fought desperately and savagely to the bitter end. As casualties increased, so did the demand for nurses. In early 1945 to address this need, President Roosevelt proposed a nursing draft unless an additional 18,000 volunteered. Since 9,000 applications of black nurses were ignored, civil rights groups and the National Association of Colored Graduate Nurses made their displeasure known. Outspoken and influential Harlem area Congressman **Adam Clayton Powell** expressed his impatience with this decision as well:

> It is absolutely unbelievable that in times like these, when the world is going forward, that there are leaders in our American life who are going backward. It is further unbelievable that these leaders have become so blindly and unreasonably un-American that they have forced our wounded men to face the tragedy of death rather than allow trained nurses to aid because these nurses skins happen to be of a different color.

In the end, the proposal to draft nurses never passed Congress. In January of 1945, the army finally admitted African American women into the Nurse Corps. The navy soon followed. Only 500 African American nurses were allowed to serve in the war compared to 59,000 white nurses.

Head of the nursing staff at Camp Beal, CA. Captain Raney. (Source: *National Archives*)

Final Thoughts

The black experience in World War II would profoundly change the course of the United States and race relations for decades to come. The seeds that blossomed in the 1950's and 60's Civil Rights movement were planted during this time, and African American women played a key role in making that happen. Indeed, some of the major players of the Civil Rights movement got much needed experience during this time that would prove to be valuable down the road. It was during the WWII years that Rosa Parks and Jackie Robinson on a military base first challenged segregated seating on transportation and that Thurgood Marshall sharpened his skills in courtrooms. Civil Rights organizations such as the NAACP formulated the legal strategy that would eventually topple segregation in American life. During the war years, African Americans made a conscious decision to no longer passively accept a supporting role in their own mistreatment and discrimination. They challenged Jim Crow practices in the military and mobilized to fight two wars. Racism at home was just as dangerous to a black man or woman as fighting Fascism overseas. The black female experience, as chronicled in this book and other works, show that they were up to the challenge, and would not take no for an answer. They demonstrated that being confined to the kitchen or the cotton field vastly underestimated their skill and humanity. They could not live where they wanted, vote in many states, or sit where they wanted to sit on the bus, but they helped to win a war. They persisted. They challenged. They petitioned. They sued. But most of all they opened doors that their children and grandchildren could walk through. They deserve the highest honor this nation can bestow.

Most histories credit the women's rights movement as a phenomenon of the 1960's-70's, but clearly their sisters who fought in the trenches of racism and sexism in the 1940's served as inspiration.

Interview with Ruth Wilson

At the time that Mrs. Wilson agreed to talk to me she was 99 years old. This interview was conducted in October of 2021.

1. What was your work experience during the war? *I worked on the U.S.S. Valley forge. I was a Sheet Metal worker at the Philadelphia Navy yard*
2. How did you become a Sheet Metal worker? *I was working in laundry at the Navy yard. I quit because they wanted me to work during my lunch hour. I got a letter from the federal government telling me that I can't quit during war, so they sent me to Sheet Metal School for about 6 weeks. After the 6 weeks I was sent to the Navy yard. I had to take a test prior to being sent to school.*
3. Did you experience any racism?
   Of course there was racism, but I kept on going because I was used to it. There was a Jewish mechanic that was like a father figure to me.
4. What were some examples of the racism you experienced? *The ladies room. They would use paper towels to touch the door. They didn't want to have to use it behind you. Whispering amongst themselves.*
5. Tell me more about your work experience?
   I think I worked around 8 hours a day. I put in the bulkheads on the ship. The ship could carry around 100 planes.
6. Did you have pride in what you were doing? *I was proud of it, but at the time it was just a job. But I appreciate it more now. I made more money than I ever made.*

Interview with Professor Gregory Cooke

I had the opportunity to talk to one of the leading scholars of the "Black Rosies" and of the African-American experience in World War II. He has researched and documented this history for over 30 years. He has an upcoming documentary on the Black Rosies entitled "Invisible Warriors: African-American Women in World War II." Mr. Cooke is a career educator, documentary filmmaker, and World War II historian, dedicated to helping "relocate African Americans from the margins to the main pages of American and global history." Here are some edited excerpts of our conversation.

Q: How did the Black experience in WWII change history and impact the Civil Rights Movement in the years that followed?

A: *First, what we consider to be the modern Civil Rights Movement really started during WWII. You had co-eds at Howard University who did a sit-in at a lunch counter. They were arrested, booked and taken to jail. One of the Rosie's who transitioned about six years ago, by the name of Birdia Bush, worked at the War Department. In her off time, she demonstrated and picketed movie theaters and restaurants that did not let black people in. So this type of activism that people usually equate with the 1950's and 60's, a lot of it really started during WWII. Additionally, during WWII there were approximately 1.1 million African American men and women that served in all branches of the military, so after having had that experience there was a sense that we are entitled to full participation economically, legally, etc. There was this feeling that they had earned the right to full citizenship. The whole back of the bus and not being able to vote had worn thin at this point....*

By the time Rosa Parks did her thing in 1955, we are now talking 10 years after the end of WWII, and many of the men and women, were right out of highschool during the war, maybe 19, 20 and 21; so ten years after the war they were now grown men and women, so they were prepared to take on the challenges of fighting for equality.

You have icons of the Civil Rights Movement like Medgar Evers and Ralph Abernathy who were in the military during WWII.....One of the biggest things that contributed was that black men and women served with distinction in WWII, and as a result of that President Harry S. Truman issued the executive order in 1948 that ended racial segregation in the US military....."

One of the other things that happened that was real big was that you had more than a half a million African Americans that left the country during WWII. Most of those went to Europe, particularly Great Britain. For the most part white British civilians treated them as equals, as Americans and as human beings. They had this interaction with whites that they couldn't of possibly had in the US. They were invited into their homes for dinner, into their churches, they went to dances...they saw that all white people were not like the white people in America, and so it broadened their perspective on what the possibilities could be. They brought a lot of that back with them to America of being treated as equals by whites.

Additionally, when you look at 1.1 million blacks in the military, minimally they were making around $55 a month, which was a large sum of money in the 1940's. This was more than what black people had ever made. In the military you did have equality in terms of rank and pay. This equality of pay did not exist in American society. When you *combine the 1.1 million with the 600,000, now you have 1.7 million black people who had economic opportunity for the first time which was the largest instance in our history up to that point....that had a tremendous impact on the black community....Even though many blacks did not receive benefits from the G.I. Bill, the ones that did went to HBCU's and that had a big impact in building the postwar-black middle class.*

If you look at World War II, to my knowledge we basically had three fabrics: wool, cotton, and silk. Those hundreds of thousands of black people trapped in the Sharecropping system were planting, nurturing, and harvesting cotton. So cotton played a huge role in the war effort. If we want to get technical, we have to expand the definition of Rosie's to include the farmers.

Q: The title of your upcoming documentary is entitled "Invisible Warriors." Why are they considered "Invisible Warriors?"

Because during the war, they were not focused upon. There were 600,000 of these women and to my knowledge I have never seen a recruitment poster trying to get black women. During the war, black women were the last hired and the first fired. Blacks were largely edited out of the experience......600,000 is a big number about anything. And if you were to put all 600,000 in one city, based on the 1940 census, they would've been the 13th largest city in America. They played a critical role in helping to win the war, but I feel like it's only now that black women are having a big cultural impact unlike any time before, partially because of social media and people like you and the work I'm doing to bring this to the forefront...There is more visibility now than when I started this project. They were warriors of a different type. They weren't on the battlefield, but without them America would've had a difficult time winning World War II and without the help of 8 million American women of all stripes....

Q: **What barriers did African American women face in becoming full participants in the war effort?** *There were two things going on: there was racism (Jim Crow, segregation, racial violence and all that went with being black) and then there was the gender issue with black and white women. They were going into jobs that were exclusively white male: welder, riveter, etc...They were going into these new places and often they were not treated well. They were not greeted with the kind of enthusiasm or support they should've been. There were stereotypes about black women having venereal diseases. One of the most famous cases happened at Baltimore Western Electric (see page 16). My research several years ago indicated that the plumbing codes of Baltimore city actually required the separation of races. There was a critical labor shortage throughout World War II, and in many cases employers refused to hire black women because they feared that their white employees would quit, or that white women would go on strike because of the refusal to share restroom facilities with black women.*

Q: What motivated you to pursue this topic on Black Rosies?

I've been on World War II as it relates to black folks going on 34 years this Veterans Day. Thirty-four years ago I was spiritually compelled to go to Bastogne, Belgium. It just happened to be the 70th anniversary of the end of World War I. I go to Bastogne and go to this museum, and there were black soldiers in the diorama. It was the first time in my life that I had ever seen black people in a museum in the military in World War II, and it blew me away. As a result of that, I started reading everything I could about black people in World War II. Mostly I focused on Europe, so that took me to Great Britain. When I went to Great Britain and looked at the African-American presence there, I stumbled upon the British version of Rosie the Riveter and then that took me back to Rosie the Riveter in America. That's how I came upon the Black Rosies. I had never heard of them before and I also had this bias of when I think of war, I think of men....I realized when I was growing up (around 3-4 years old) my mother used to tell me this story about how she rode on her suitcase from Norfolk, Virginia to Washington, D.C. to get her very first job as a clerk typist in the U.S. Patent Office. She didn't tell me that she rode on a Jim Crow train car. She didn't tell me it was World War II. But the reason I remembered the story was because it had a train in it, and I had a lifelong love of trains. I remembered that because she told me the story several times. She was 18 years old. That's when I started saying, "Wow! There's something here, and my mother was involved." My mother transitioned in 2006, so that's when I started this work. I suspect she went to her grave not knowing her historical significance either."

About the Author

Dante R. Brizill has been a social studies educator for the last 18 years in Maryland and Delaware. He earned a Bachelor's degree in history from Hampton University in Virginia and a Masters of Arts in Teaching from Wesley College in Delaware. A native of Philadelphia, he is a die-hard fan of the Philadelphia Eagles. His hobbies include reading, writing and traveling. He resides in Delaware with his wife and children. A lifelong history buff, Brizill has always been passionate about helping young people recognize the contributions of all Americans. In 2018 he achieved a life-long dream of writing and publishing his first book, *Dorie Miller: Greatness Under Fire*. Since the publication of that book, the U.S. Navy announced that it would be building an aircraft carrier in his honor. Brizill followed up in 2020 with the publication of *Red Ball Express: Greatness Under Fire.* His writings have appeared in the *Delaware News Journal*, *Historynet.com*, the *Cecil Whig*, the *Richmond-Times Dispatch*, the *Dallas Morning News*, the *Philadelphia Inquirer*, and *WWII Quarterly*. He has also appeared on Fox 45 Baltimore, WJBR, Delaware Public Radio, and Maryland Public radio. Currently he is a proud member of the faculty of POLYTECH High School in Delaware.

About the book cover designer

Robert Gussio has over 40 years of experience in the area of art. At a young age, he discovered his love for drawing and sketching but did not take it seriously even into his teen years. He has studied his craft privately, in college, and at the Schuler School of Fine Arts under the instruction of Ann Didusch Shuler. He has contributed to numerous publications integrating fine arts and graphics. Although he mostly considers himself to an unapologetic pragmatist, he occasionally accepts jobs exercising his illustrative skills working with oil paint, pen and ink, and mixed media, contingent on the project. He resides in the Baltimore area. Mr. Gussio also designed the cover for *Dorie Miller: Greatness Under Fire* and *Red Ball Express: Greatness Under Fire.* Feel free to visit **rggraphics.net** for examples of his work.

Glossary of Key Terms and People

WACs- Women's Army Corps

Major Charity Adams Earley- She commanded the 6888th Central Postal Directory Battalion. She was the highest ranking African American woman in WWII.

Eleanor Roosevelt- Wife of President Franklin D. Roosevelt. Served as First Lady from 1933-1945. She was a key ally to full racial equality in America, and used her clout with the President and contacts to help move the things forward.

Mary McCleod Bethune- Educator and civil rights activist. Founder of Bethune-Cookman college. Adviser to President Roosevelt and a friend of First Lady Eleanor Roosevelt. Pushed heavily for African-American women to be included as active participants in the war.

Mable K. Staupers- the executive secretary of the National Association of Colored Nurses who lobbied for a change in the policy that excluded black women nurses in World War II.

Adam Clayton Powell- Influential and powerful African-American congressman and civil rights activist that represented Harlem for over two decades in the House of Representatives.

Let's Review

Discuss the following questions with someone who has read the book, your classmates, or book club:

1. **What challenges did African American women encounter in being full participants in our nations struggle to win World War II?**

2. **How did they overcome these challenges?**

3. **Why was Congressman Adam Clayton Powell upset about the plan to draft nurses?**

4. **Why were African-American women finally accepted into the nursing program?**

5. **Why were African-American women disappointed in their assignment to care for German POW's? Do you think they were right to feel this way? Explain.**

6. **How did Ruth Wilson end up working on the** *U.S.S. Valley Forge?*

7. **In the interview, Ruth Wilson indicated that she received a letter explaining that she could not quit during war. Why do you think that was told to her?**

Extend Your Learning

1. **Pretend that you are a reporter that is interviewing a black woman worker in a defense factory during World War II. Create five questions and five answers they would have given based on what you have learned.**

2. **Research the court cases of Effie Mae Turner and Claretta Johnson. On what basis did their lawyers argue as to why they should be hired? Why did the courts rule the way that they did?**

3. **Ruth Wilson worked on the *U.S.S. Valley Forge*. Research the role that ship had in World War II.**

4. **When did it become illegal for employers to discriminate based on race and gender in the United States? How did the experience of the Black Rosies in World War II help lead to this?**

5. **Gregory Cooke indicated that his own mother may have went to her grave not understanding her "historical significance." Do you believe this was true of most Black Rosies? Explain.**

6. **Research the friendship between First Lady Eleanor Roosevelt and Mary McLeod Bethune. How did their friendship help to advance the cause of racial and gender equality?**

Bibliography and Recommended Reading

Books:

1. Honey, Maureen *Bitter Fruit: African American Women in World War II.* University of Missouri Press, 1999.
2. Mullenbach, Cheryl *Double Victory.* Chicago Review Press, 2017.
3. Berry, Daina and Gross, Kali *A Black Women's History of the United States.* Beacon Press, 2020.

Articles:

1. Alexis Clark (2018) "The Army's First Black Nurses Were Relegated to Caring for Nazi Prisoners of War"
2. Aaron Randle (2020) "Black Rosies: The Forgotten African-American Heroines of the World War II Homefront."

Acknowledgements

I would like to take this opportunity to thank God for giving me a purpose to tell these stories about the "Black Rosies". I would like to thank my editor Nancy Samuels for her patience and dedication. Once again my cover designer Bob Gussio hit the ball out of the park with an amazing cover that is historically accurate and honors the service of the women. The National Archives and its wealth of materials and pictures has always been valuable to my research. My publicist, Ray Feldmann, for understanding the vision and the passion I have for these stories and for helping to promote my Greatness Under Fire series to the general public. I would also like to acknowledge Ruth Wilson one of the "Black Rosies" who worked in my hometown of Philadelphia. It was amazing to speak with her. Professor Cooke of Drexel University has been invaluable to this project with his advice, pointers and contacts. He provided the icing on the cake that was needed for this project. I must acknowledge my wife, family, friends, students, former students, and colleagues who have encouraged me over these past few years to keep telling these stories. My heart is full of gratitude to everyone who has helped to make this "Greatness Under Fire" series a reality.

Also by the author:

From the back cover: "He was the ship's cook. He wasn't trained on how to operate the weapons on his ship, only on how to pass ammunition. But on December 7th, 1941, Dorie Miller showed his country that he was capable of much more. This is his story. Read it and be inspired!

"Every American should know about Dorie Miller. Brizill does a great job of both setting the historical context and telling the story of Miller's heroism at Pearl Harbor. I couldn't agree more with Brizill's last line-"Let's keep this story alive!"- ***Steve Sheinkin, author of The Port Chicago 50***

From the back cover: "In the second installment of Brizill's *Greatness Under Fire* series, we learn about the courage and heroics of these essential men of World War II......All heroes don't wear capes. Some drive trucks."

"Brizill has remarkably synthesized a lost story that should be included in the history curriculum......I am grateful that the story of the Red Ball Express did not go away just because we stopped talking about it." **- *Virginia Rector, Educator and author of "How Can I serve You?"***

Made in the USA
Middletown, DE
13 March 2022